Peek-A-Boo, I See You

by Sarah Holliday

Copyright © by Harcourt Brace & Company

All rights reserved. No part of this publication may be reproduced or transmitted in any form or by any means, electronic or mechanical, including photocopy, recording, or any information storage and retrieval system.

Teachers using SIGNATURES may photocopy complete pages in sufficient quantities for classroom use only and not for resale.

HARCOURT BRACE and Quill Design is a registered trademark of Harcourt Brace & Company.

Printed in the United States of America

ISBN 0-15-314547-1

Ordering Options
ISBN 0-15-314559-5 (Grade K Collection)
ISBN 0-15-314560-9 (package of 5)

Harcourt Brace School Publishers

3 4 5 6 7 8 9 10 179 2002 2001

L

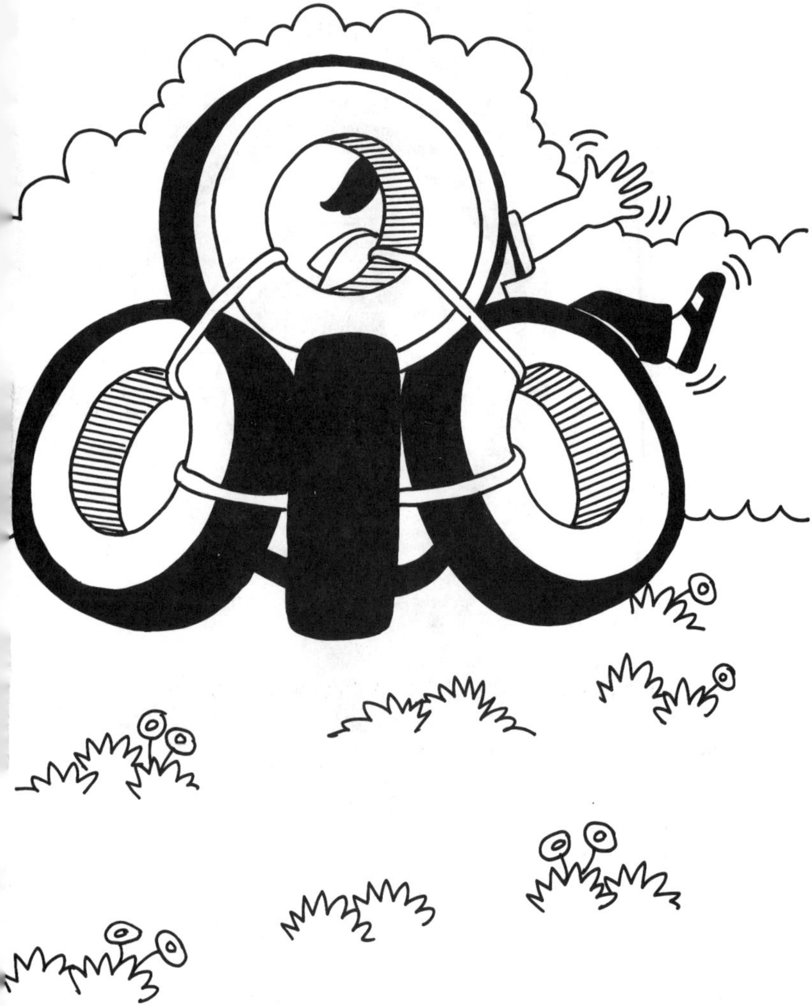

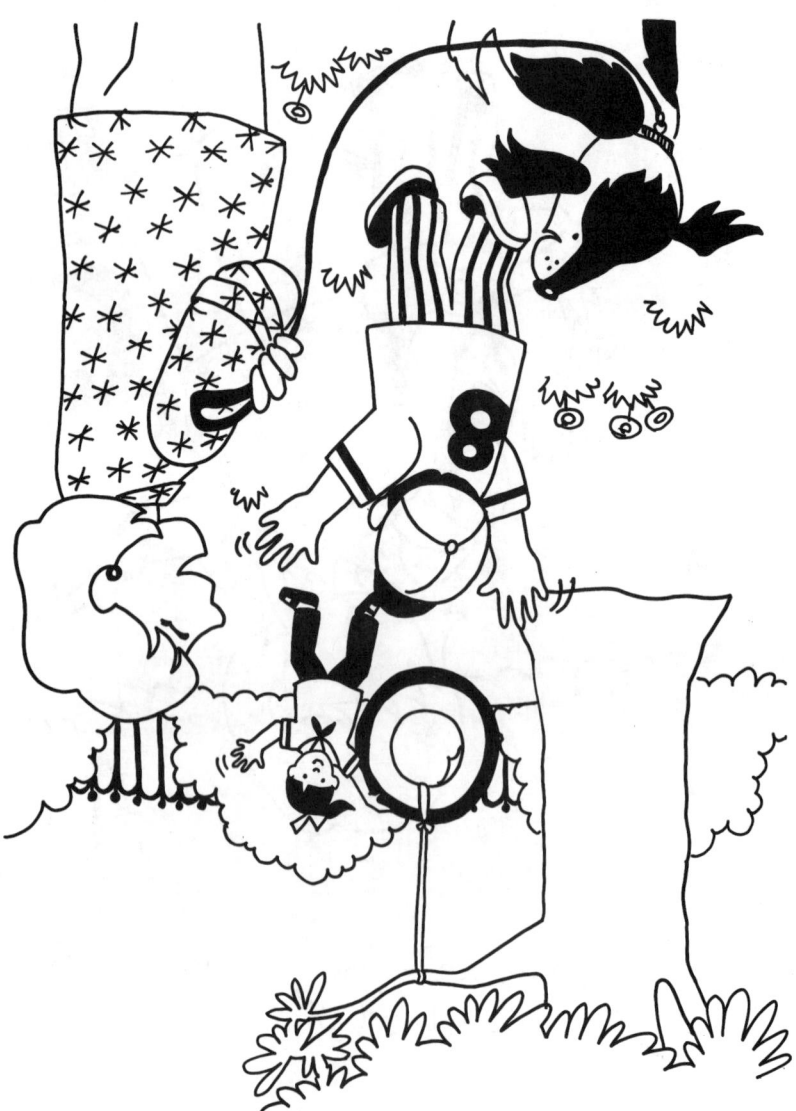

TAKE-HOME BOOK
Use with "Dancing Feet."